THE FUNNIEST SPOOKY JOKE BOOK EVER

THE FUNNIEST SPOOKY JOKE BOOK EVER

By Joe King

Illustrated by Nigel Baines

Andersen Press

This edition first published in Great Britain in 2011 by
ANDERSEN PRESS LIMITED
20 Vauxhall Bridge Road
London SW1V 2SA
www.andersenpress.co.uk

Reprinted 2012, 2013

British Library Cataloguing in
Publication Data available.

ISBN 978 1 84939 301 0

Printed and bound in Great Britain by
Clays Limited, Bungay, Suffolk, NR35 1ED

GHOSTLY GAGS

Where do baby ghosts go during the day?
Dayscare centres

What do you get when you cross Bambi with a ghost?
Bamboo

What are little ghosts dressed in when it rains?
Boo-ts and ghoul-oshes

What is a little ghost's favourite game?
Peek-a-boo

What do you call a ghost's mother and father?
Transparents

What did the polite ghost say to her son?
'Don't spook until your spooken to.'

What story do little ghosts like to hear at bedtime?
Ghouldelocks and the Three Scares

**What did the ghost
teacher say to her class?**
*'Watch the board and
I'll go through it again.'*

**What kind of mistakes do
spooks make at school?**
Boo boos

**What's a young ghost's
favourite ride at the fair?**
The roller ghoster

**What did the mother ghost
say to the baby ghost?**
'Put your shocks and boos on.'

Where do ghosts buy their food?
At the ghost-ery shop

**When does a ghost
have breakfast?**
In the moaning

**What do ghosts eat
for breakfast?**
Dreaded wheat

**What do ghosts drink
at breakfast?**
Coffee with scream and sugar

What do ghosts eat for lunch?
Ghoulash

What do ghosts eat for dinner?
Spook-ghetti

**What is a ghost's
favourite dessert?**
Boo-Berry pie with I-scream

**What tops off a ghost's
ice-cream sundae?**
Whipped scream

What is a ghost's favourite fruit?
Booberries

**Why is a ghost such
a messy eater?**
Because he is always goblin

**What do you call a
demon who slurps his food?**
A goblin

**What do demons have
for breakfast?**
Devilled eggs

What do ghosts dance to?
Soul music

**Who did the ghost
invite to his party?**
Anyone he could dig up

**Why was the young ghost's
birthday party so noisy?**
*His friends gave him the bumps in
the night*

**Who did the ghost go with
to the Halloween party?**
With No-body

**What is a ghost's favourite
party game?**
Hide-and-shriek

**Where does a ghost go
on Saturday night?**
Anywhere where he can boo-gie

**What kind of tie does a ghost
wear to a formal party?**
A boo-tie

**Why do ghosts and demons
get along so well?**
*Because demons are a ghost's
best friend*

**What did the boy ghost
say to the girl ghost?**
You look boo-tiful tonight

How do ghosts fall in love?
It's love at first fright

**Where do ghosts send
their letters?**
At the ghost office

**What kind of street does
a ghost like best?**
A dead end

Where do ghosts live?
In a terrortory

**Why are ghosts bad
at telling lies?**
*Because you can see
right through them*

**What do you call a ghost
with a broken leg?**
Hoblin Goblin

**What do you call
a prehistoric ghost?**
A terror-dactyl

**Who speaks at the ghosts'
press conference?**
The spooksperson

**What should you say when you
meet a ghost?**
How do you boo, sir?

What goes boo, putt putt putt, boo, putt putt putt?
A ghost playing golf

Who's the most important member of a ghost's football team?
The ghoulie

Who was the famous ghost detective?
Sherlock Moans

**What kind of ghost
has the best hearing?**
The eeriest

Where do ghosts swim?
The Dead Sea

What is a ghost's favourite bird?
A scare crow

**What did one ghost
say to another?**
'Do you believe in people?'

Why are ghosts cowards?
Because they've got no guts

Why are ghosts so popular?
They raise everybody's spirit

**What's the first thing ghosts do
when they get in a car?**
They boo-kle their seatbelts

What do ghosts use to clean
their hair?
Shamboo

Knock, knock
Who's there
Boo
Boo, who?
Please don't cry

Why won't the ghost read the
book about a graveyard?
He doesn't like the plot

On what day do ghosts make the
most noise?
Moan-day

What happens when a ghost
gets lost in the fog?
He is mist

Why do ghosts shiver and moan?
It's drafty under that sheet

**How can you tell when
a ghost is scared?**
He goes as white as a sheet

**What happens when a
ghost gets a fright?**
He jumps into his skin

**How do ghosts check that their
paintings hang straight?**
With a spirit level

**How do ghost hunters
keep in touch?**
By eeeeek-mail

**Did you hear about the really
rotten spook?**
He was a ghastly ghost

**What do short-sighted
ghosts wear?**
Spooktacles

Did you hear about the deadly comedian?
He was dead funny

**What do you call a ghost
with an upset stomach?**
Spew-ky

**What is the demons'
favourite TV sitcom?**
Fiends

**What do demons
have on holiday?**
A devil of a time

**What is a devils'
picket line called?**
A demonstration

What trees do ghouls like best?
Ceme-trees

**How can you tell if a
corpse is angry?**
It flips its lid

How do undertakers speak?
Gravely

**What do young ghouls write
their homework in?**
Exorcise books

Who writes ghost jokes?
Crypt writers

**Why did the car stop
when it saw a ghost?**
It had a nervous breakdown

Where do ghost trains stop?
At devil crossings

**A woman wanted
to marry a ghost.**
I don't know what possessed her

**What happened when the
ghost asked for a whiskey
at his local bar?**
*The bartender said, 'Sorry sir,
we don't serve spirits here.'*

MONSTER MAYHEM

What kind of monster likes to dance?
The boogieman

What did the girl say when the monster doctor asked to look inside her mouth?
Arrrrrggggggghhhhhh!

**What do you shout
when the Abominable
Snowman surprises you?**
Not Yeti ...

**What's the best way to
speak to a monster?**
From a long way away

What did the monster say when he accidentally sat on a packet of biscuits?
Crumbs!

Where do Zombies go on holiday?
The Deaditerranean

What is the Loch Ness Monster's favourite takeaway meal?
Fish 'n' ships

What does a monster become after it's a year old?
Two years old

Why do dragons sleep all day?
So they can fight knights

What do monsters eat for pudding?
Eyes-cream

Why don't monsters eat nuclear power stations?
They give them atomic-ache

How did the Hunchback of Notre Dame cure his sore throat?
He gargoyled

**What time is it when a
monster sits on your bike?**
Time to get a new bike

**What do you say when you
meet a three-headed monster?**
Hello, hello, hello

**What do monster mums do
with cars, buses and trucks?**
They make a traffic jam

**What do hairy monsters
eat for pudding?**
Lice cream

**What flavour squash did the
monster like to slurp?**
Lemon and slime

**How do monsters
cook their food?**
They terror-fry it

**Which soaps do monsters
love to watch?**
Beastenders and Coronation Screech

**What do you say to a monster
with a dribbly nose?**
Goo away

**What happens when you
throw a warty, stinky
monster in the Dead Sea?**
It gets wet

**What steps should you take
if an axe-wielding ogre
gallops towards you?**
Great big ones

**What do you get if you cross
the Abominable Snowman
with a vampire?**
Frostbite

**What happens when an ogre sits
in front of you at the cinema?**
You miss most of the film

**Who won the ogres's
beauty contest?**
No one

MISS SWAMPY

**How does an ogre count
to twenty-three?**
On his fingers

**Why did the monster leave a
dirty ring around the bath?**
It was just scum

**What do you call someone
who likes to pick his
nose under the bed?**
The bogeyman

**Which sculpture came last in the
snowman-building competition?**
The Abominable Snowman

**What do you call a three-headed
monster with stinky cheese in
all six of his hairy ears?**
Anything you like – he can't hear you

**Why did the monster
cross the road?**
*To show the other
monsters he had guts*

**What happened at the
monster's wedding party?**
They toasted the bride and groom

When do monsters cook you?
On Fried-days

**How can you help a
starving monster?**
Give them a hand

**What does a monster
call a skateboarder?**
Meals on wheels

What's the definition of an ogre?
*Someone who goes into a
restaurant and orders a waiter*

**What did the monster
say when he was full?**
'I couldn't eat another mortal.'

**What did the Abominable
Snowman say to the explorer?**
'Nice to meat you.'

**Why don't monsters
eat weathermen?**
Because they give them wind

**What did the ogre say
when he saw Snow White
and the seven dwarfs?**
'Lunch'

**What happened when
Dr Frankenstein
cloned his monster?**
The monster was beside himself

**Why was Frankenstein's
monster late for the party?**
*He couldn't pull himself
together in time*

What did the monster eat after the dentist pulled its tooth?
The dentist

What would you do if you opened the front door and saw Dracula, Frankenstein's monster, three ghosts, a werewolf and eight witches standing on the doorstep?
Hope it was Halloween

What would you get if a monster stepped on Batman and Robin?
Flatman and Ribbon

What happened to the monster who swallowed a whole chicken farm?
He was in a fowl mood all day

Did Frankenstein make his monster laugh?
Yes, he kept him in stitches

**How do you open
a haunted house?**
With a skeleton key

**What's spookier than the
outside of a haunted house?**
The inside

**What do mummies do
on the weekends?**
They unwind

**What did *The Mummy*
film director say when
the final scene was done?**
'OK, that's a wrap.'

**When do monster
mothers receive gifts?**
On mummy's day

**Why couldn't the mummy
answer the telephone?**
Because it was all tied up

RING
RING

**What do mummies talk about
when they get together?**
Old times

**Where does the monster
keep his hands?**
In a handbag

**What do ghosts say when
something is really great?**
Ghoul

**What can't you give
the headless horseman?**
A headache

SKELETON SCREAMERS

What do skeletons say before they begin dining?
Bone appétit

34

When does a skeleton laugh?
*When something tickles
its funny bone*

**Why didn't the skeleton dance
at the Halloween party?**
It had no body to dance with

**What type of art
do skeletons like?**
Skull-tures

What did the skeleton say when his brother told a lie?
'You can't fool me, I can see right through you.'

What did the skeleton say while riding his Harley-Davidson motorcycle?
'I'm bone to be wild!'

Who was the most famous French skeleton?
Napoleon bone-apart

**What instrument do
skeletons play?**
Trom-bone

**What does a skeleton
order at a restaurant?**
Spare ribs

**Why are skeletons
usually so calm?**
Nothing gets under their skin

Why are graveyards so noisy?
Because of all the coffin

**How did the skeleton know it
was going to rain?**
He could feel it in his bones

**How do skeletons call
their friends?**
On the telebone

What do you call a skeleton who won't get up in the morning?
Lazy bones

What do you call a stupid skeleton?
Bonehead

**Why didn't the skeleton
want to play football?**
Because his heart wasn't in it

**Why didn't the skeleton
play church music?**
He had no organs

**Why didn't the skeleton
cross the road?**
He didn't have the guts

Why are skeletons so lazy?
They're bone idle

**'Skeletons please, all be seated,
I don't want this to be repeated,
I've gathered you here
to announce, with a tear:
I've never once been trick or
treated!'**

FANGTASTIC VAMPIRE JOKES

What has webbed feet, feathers and fangs, and goes *quack quack*?
Count Duckula

What is Transylvania?
Dracula's terror-tory

**What kind of ship
does Dracula own?**
A blood vessel

**Why doesn't anyone
like Count Dracula?**
He's a pain in the neck

**What does Dracula say when
he's introduced to someone?**
'Hello, pleased to eat you.'

**What is a vampire's
favourite fruit?**
A neck-tarine

**Who did Dracula take
out on a date?**
His ghoul friend

**What is the best way to
talk to Count Dracula?**
Long distance

How does a girl vampire flirt?
She bats her eyes

**What do you give
a vampire with a cold?**
Coffin drops

**What did the teacher say
to Dracula after he failed his
maths test?**
'Can't you count Dracula?'

**Where do vampires
go on holiday?**
The Isle of Fright

**Who plays centre forward for
the vampire football team?**
The ghoulscorer

**What happened at
the vampires' race?**
It finished neck and neck

**What do vampires
sing on New Year's Eve?**
Auld Fang Syne

**What flavour ice cream
is Dracula's favourite?**
Veinilla

**What happened to the
mad vampire?**
He went a little batty

**How does a vampire like his
food served?**
In bite-sized pieces

**Which vampire tried
to eat James Bond?**
Ghouldfinger

**What do you get if you cross
Dracula and Al Capone?**
A fangster

**What does the postman
deliver to vampires?**
Fang mail

Knock, knock
Who's there?
Discount
Discount, who?
Discount is named Dracula

Why does Dracula brush his teeth after every meal?
To avoid bat-breath

What happened when the vampire began to write poetry?
He went from bat to verse

Why is Dracula able to live so cheaply?
He lives on necks to nothing

What should you never say if you are being chased by Dracula?
I give up.
Exactly.

Why are vampires the most unhappy creatures?
Because they always love in vein

**Why doesn't Dracula give
up being a vampire?**
He can't, it's in his blood

**Where does Dracula do
most of his singing?**
In the bat-tub

**Why did the vampire do
so badly at school?**
He didn't have the right battitude

Why doesn't Dracula marry?
He's a confirmed bat-chelor

**Is it true that you can escape
from Dracula if you carry a
clove of garlic with you?**
*Yes, if you can carry the
clove of garlic fast enough*

**Why should you avoid
vampires at dawn?**
*Because they like a quick
bite before they go to bed*

**What's the difference between
a vampire with a sore tooth
and a stormy day?**
*One roars with pain, the
other pours with rain*

**What would you get
if you crossed a vampire
bat and a magician?**
A flying sorcerer

**What did the skeleton
say to the vampire?**
'You suck.'

**Why was the girl
afraid of the vampire?**
He was all bite and no bark

**Why doesn't Dracula mind the
doctor looking at his throat?**
Because of the coffin

**How can you tell if a
vampire likes baseball?**
Every night he turns into a bat

**What do you call a
blood-sucking vampire
who tells fantastic jokes?**
Horribly funny

**What do you call a vampire
who likes to relax in a
bloodbath with a good book?**
Well red

**Where do vampires
keep their savings?**
In a blood bank

**Did you hear about the
vampire who needed a drink?**
He was bloodthirsty

**Why do vampires
like thick books?**
*They like a story they
can get their teeth in to*

How did Dracula play cricket?
With a vampire bat

**On one frightening
Halloween night,
A tall vampire
Threatened to bite.
The ghouls danced about
While zombies gave shout,
And the ghosts flitted
By with delight.**

WEREWOLF HOWLERS

Who are some of the werewolves' cousins?
The whatwolves and whenwolves

What happened when the werewolf chewed a bone for an hour?
When he got up he only had three legs

**How do you make
a werewolf stew?**
Keep him waiting for two hours

**What happens if you cross a
werewolf and a sheep**
You have to get a new sheep

**What is fearsome, hairy and
drinks from the wrong side
of a glass?**
A werewolf with hiccups

**What happened when the
werewolf swallowed a clock?**
He got ticks

William: Mother, all the children make fun of me.
Mother: What do they say?
William: They say I'm a werewolf. Is it true?
Mother: Of course not. Now comb your face and get ready for supper.

What kind of beans do werewolves like?
Human beans

Why does the werewolf sleep all day long?
Who wants to wake him up?

Why did the werewolf finally take a bath?
He decided to give up his life of grime

How was the werewolf's birthday party?
It was a howling success

**What do you get if you
cross a werewolf with a tree?**
*A tree whose bark is as
good as its bite*

**What kind of fur do you
get from a werewolf?**
As fur as you can get

**Which scary creature
is always getting lost?**
A where-wolf

WITCH
CACKLERS

**Why don't angry witches
ride their brooms?**
*They're afraid of flying
off the handle*

AAIIIIEEEE!

**How does the witch know
what time it is?**
She looks at her witch-watch

**What is a witch's
favourite subject at school?**
Spelling

**Why do witches
wear name tags?**
So they know which witch is which

**What do you call two
witches living together?**
Broom mates

**What does a witch ask
for when she is in a hotel?**
Broom service

**What do you call a witch
who lives at the beach?**
A sand-witch

What noise does a witch's breakfast cereal make?
Snap, cackle and pop

What do you get if you cross a witch and an iceberg?
A cold spell

What do you call a witch by the side of the road with her thumb out?
A witchhiker

**Why did the witch put her
broom in the wash?**
She wanted a clean sweep

What has six legs and flies?
A witch giving her cat a ride

**What do you call a
witch with one leg?**
Eileen

**What is the difference between a
musician and a dead witch?**
*One composes and the
other decomposes*

**What do you get if you
cross an owl with a witch?**
*A bird that's ugly but doesn't
give a hoot*

**Why won't a witch
wear a flat hat?**
Because there is no point in it

What goes cackle, cackle, bonk?
A witch laughing her head off

What do you call a nervous witch?
A twitch

How do you make a witch itch?
Take away the 'w'

**What kind of tests do they
set at witch school?**
Hex-aminations

**Why didn't the witch
sing at the concert?**
Because she had a frog in her throat

**What happened to the naughty
little witch at school?**
She was ex-spelled

**Why should men beware of
beautiful witches?**
They'll sweep them off their feet

**What did the black cat
say to the fish?**
I've got a bone to pick with you

What do witches' cats strive for?
Purrfection

**What is evil, ugly and black,
and goes round and round?**
A witch in a revolving door

**What happens if you
see twin witches?**
*You won't be able to tell
which witch is which*

**What happened to the wizard
who ran away with the circus?**
*The police made him
bring it back again*

**What do you get if you cross a
dinosaur with a wizard?**
Tyrannosaurus hex

**What do witches read
in the newspaper?**
Their horrorscopes

**Witch: 'Do you want to go
dancing tonight?"**
*Zombie: 'Not tonight,
I'm dead on my feet.'*

Knock, knock
Who's there?
Witch
Witch who?
Bless you

**What did the witch say
when she met the
two-headed monster?**
*'Hello, hello.
How are you? How are you?'*

**Witch 1: 'Are you really going
to meet that vampire?"**
*Witch 2: 'I was, but I'm beginning to
experience grave doubts.'*

What does a witch say to her broom at bed time?
Go to sweep

What do witches put on their hair?
Scare-spray

How does a witch travel when she doesn't have a broom?
She witch-hikes

What do you call a wizard with a furry face and a lightening-shaped scar?
Hairy Potter

What do you call a wizard with a furry face and a lightening-shaped scar who shouts boo?
Hairy Scary Potter

**Which part of a roast pork
dinner do witches like best?**
The cackling

**Did you know witches have a
bad sense of direction?**
Now, which way is it?

**Wanda the witch, on her broom,
swept through the town yelling,
'ZOOM!'
Through a perchance of luck
never heard the big truck
and she zoomed on her broom
to her doom.**

GRAVE-STONES

Why was there a road into the
cemetery, but no road out of it?
It was a dead end